# 50 Vegan Wraps and Burritos Recipes

By: Kelly Johnson

# Table of Contents

- Classic Veggie Burrito
- Spicy Chickpea Wrap
- Tofu and Avocado Wrap
- Sweet Potato and Black Bean Burrito
- BBQ Tempeh Wrap
- Grilled Veggie Wrap with Tahini Sauce
- Cauliflower and Chickpea Burrito
- Lentil and Spinach Wrap
- Roasted Vegetable and Hummus Wrap
- Mushroom and Kale Burrito
- Mexican Rice and Bean Wrap
- Tempeh Bacon and Avocado Wrap
- Falafel Wrap with Tzatziki
- Grilled Portobello Mushroom Burrito
- Peanut Butter and Banana Wrap
- Sweet Potato, Quinoa, and Black Bean Wrap
- Curry Chickpea Wrap
- Avocado and Cucumber Sushi Roll Wrap
- Cauliflower Buffalo Wrap
- Zucchini and Hummus Wrap
- Eggplant and Tomato Burrito
- Spicy Sriracha Tofu Wrap
- Rice Paper Veggie Wrap
- Tofu Scramble and Avocado Wrap
- Grilled Corn and Avocado Burrito
- Roasted Butternut Squash Wrap
- Cabbage and Carrot Slaw Wrap
- Asian-Inspired Peanut Noodle Wrap
- Chickpea Salad Wrap
- Vegan Caesar Salad Wrap
- Avocado and Mango Burrito
- Grilled Tempeh and Arugula Wrap
- Thai Peanut Veggie Burrito
- Vegan "Chicken" Caesar Wrap
- Moroccan-Spiced Chickpea Burrito

- Mushroom and Spinach Wrap
- Avocado, Bean, and Corn Wrap
- Zesty Lime and Quinoa Burrito
- Mediterranean Veggie Wrap
- Sweet and Sour Tofu Wrap
- Lemon Herb Tofu Wrap
- Spicy Pinto Bean and Avocado Wrap
- Grilled Veggie and Hummus Wrap
- Tempeh and Kale Wrap with Mustard Dressing
- Vegan BLT Wrap
- Sweet Potato and Kale Burrito
- Chickpea and Avocado Wrap
- Vegan BBQ Seitan Wrap
- Avocado, Tomato, and Chickpea Wrap
- Mango Salsa and Black Bean Burrito

**Classic Veggie Burrito**

**Ingredients:**

- 1 large flour tortilla
- 1/2 cup cooked rice
- 1/4 cup **black beans**, rinsed and drained
- 1/4 cup **corn kernels**
- 1/4 cup **diced tomatoes**
- 1/4 cup **red bell pepper**, diced
- 1/4 cup **lettuce**, shredded
- 1/4 cup **shredded cheese** (optional)
- 1 tbsp **sour cream** (optional)
- 1 tbsp salsa
- 1/4 tsp cumin
- 1/4 tsp chili powder
- **Salt and pepper** to taste

**Instructions:**

1. In a bowl, combine rice, black beans, corn, tomatoes, and red bell pepper. Season with cumin, chili powder, salt, and pepper.
2. Warm the flour tortilla in a skillet or microwave for a few seconds.
3. Spread sour cream and salsa in the center of the tortilla.
4. Add the veggie mixture on top, followed by lettuce and cheese.
5. Fold the sides of the tortilla in and roll up tightly.
6. Slice in half and serve.

## Spicy Chickpea Wrap

**Ingredients:**

- 1 large flour tortilla
- 1/2 cup cooked chickpeas
- 1/4 cup diced cucumber
- 1/4 cup shredded carrots
- 1/4 cup spinach leaves
- 1/4 tsp cumin
- 1/4 tsp paprika
- 1/4 tsp cayenne pepper (optional, for heat)
- 1 tbsp tahini sauce
- 1 tbsp sriracha sauce
- 1 tbsp lemon juice
- **Salt and pepper** to taste

**Instructions:**

1. In a bowl, mash the chickpeas slightly with a fork or potato masher.
2. Add cumin, paprika, cayenne, salt, and pepper. Mix well.
3. Warm the tortilla and spread tahini sauce evenly across the center.
4. Layer the chickpeas, cucumber, carrots, and spinach on top.
5. Drizzle with sriracha and lemon juice.
6. Roll up the tortilla, fold in the sides, and serve.

## Tofu and Avocado Wrap

**Ingredients:**

- 1 large flour tortilla
- **1/2 cup firm tofu**, pressed and sliced
- **1/2 avocado**, sliced
- **1/4 cup shredded cabbage**
- **1/4 cup cucumber**, julienned
- 1 tbsp soy sauce
- 1 tbsp sesame oil
- 1 tbsp rice vinegar
- 1 tsp sesame seeds
- **Fresh cilantro**, for garnish

**Instructions:**

1. In a pan, heat sesame oil and cook tofu slices until crispy on both sides. Drizzle with soy sauce and rice vinegar.
2. Warm the tortilla and layer with tofu, avocado, shredded cabbage, and cucumber.
3. Garnish with sesame seeds and cilantro.
4. Roll up the tortilla and slice in half.

## Sweet Potato and Black Bean Burrito

**Ingredients:**

- 1 large flour tortilla
- **1/2 cup roasted sweet potato**, diced
- **1/4 cup black beans**, rinsed and drained
- **1/4 cup corn kernels**
- **1/4 cup diced red onion**
- **1/4 cup shredded lettuce**
- **1 tbsp sour cream** (optional)
- **1 tbsp salsa**
- **1/4 tsp cumin**
- **1/4 tsp chili powder**
- **Salt and pepper** to taste

**Instructions:**

1. In a bowl, mix roasted sweet potato, black beans, corn, red onion, cumin, chili powder, salt, and pepper.
2. Warm the tortilla and spread sour cream and salsa in the center.
3. Add the veggie mixture on top, followed by shredded lettuce.
4. Roll up the burrito, fold in the sides, and serve.

## BBQ Tempeh Wrap

**Ingredients:**

- 1 large flour tortilla
- **1/2 cup tempeh**, sliced thin
- **1/4 cup BBQ sauce**
- **1/4 cup shredded cabbage**
- **1/4 cup pickled onions**
- **1/4 cup avocado**, sliced
- **1 tbsp cilantro**, chopped

**Instructions:**

1. In a pan, cook tempeh slices until golden and crispy.
2. Drizzle with BBQ sauce and cook for a few more minutes.
3. Warm the tortilla and layer with BBQ tempeh, shredded cabbage, pickled onions, and avocado.
4. Garnish with cilantro and roll up the wrap.

## Grilled Veggie Wrap with Tahini Sauce

**Ingredients:**

- 1 large flour tortilla
- 1/4 cup grilled zucchini, sliced
- 1/4 cup grilled bell peppers, sliced
- 1/4 cup grilled eggplant, sliced
- 1/4 cup spinach leaves
- 2 tbsp tahini sauce
- 1 tsp lemon juice
- Salt and pepper to taste

**Instructions:**

1. Grill the zucchini, bell peppers, and eggplant until tender.
2. Warm the tortilla and drizzle tahini sauce and lemon juice in the center.
3. Layer the grilled veggies and spinach on top.
4. Season with salt and pepper.
5. Roll up the wrap and serve.

## Cauliflower and Chickpea Burrito

**Ingredients:**

- 1 large flour tortilla
- 1/2 cup roasted cauliflower, florets
- 1/4 cup cooked chickpeas
- 1/4 cup shredded lettuce
- 1/4 cup diced tomatoes
- 1 tbsp hummus
- 1 tbsp tahini sauce
- 1/4 tsp cumin
- 1/4 tsp paprika
- **Salt and pepper** to taste

**Instructions:**

1. In a bowl, mix roasted cauliflower, chickpeas, cumin, paprika, salt, and pepper.
2. Warm the tortilla and spread hummus and tahini sauce in the center.
3. Add the cauliflower and chickpea mixture, followed by shredded lettuce and diced tomatoes.
4. Roll up the burrito and serve.

## Lentil and Spinach Wrap

**Ingredients:**

- 1 large flour tortilla
- 1/2 cup cooked lentils
- 1/4 cup cooked spinach
- 1/4 cup diced tomatoes
- 1 tbsp tahini sauce
- 1 tsp lemon juice
- 1/4 tsp cumin
- **Salt and pepper** to taste

**Instructions:**

1. In a pan, cook lentils until soft. Sauté spinach until wilted.
2. Warm the tortilla and drizzle tahini sauce and lemon juice in the center.
3. Layer the lentils, spinach, and tomatoes on top.
4. Season with cumin, salt, and pepper.
5. Roll up the wrap and serve.

## Roasted Vegetable and Hummus Wrap

**Ingredients:**

- 1 large flour tortilla
- 1/4 cup roasted carrots, sliced
- 1/4 cup roasted bell peppers, sliced
- 1/4 cup roasted zucchini, sliced
- 1/4 cup hummus
- 1 tbsp fresh parsley, chopped
- Salt and pepper to taste

**Instructions:**

1. Roast the carrots, bell peppers, and zucchini until tender.
2. Warm the tortilla and spread hummus in the center.
3. Add the roasted vegetables and sprinkle with fresh parsley.
4. Season with salt and pepper.
5. Roll up the wrap and serve.

## Mushroom and Kale Burrito

**Ingredients:**

- **1 large flour tortilla**
- **1/2 cup sautéed mushrooms**, sliced
- **1/2 cup kale**, chopped and sautéed
- **1/4 cup cooked rice**
- **1/4 cup black beans**, rinsed and drained
- **1/4 tsp garlic powder**
- **1/4 tsp smoked paprika**
- **1 tbsp tahini sauce** (optional)
- **Salt and pepper** to taste

**Instructions:**

1. Sauté mushrooms and kale in olive oil until tender. Season with garlic powder, smoked paprika, salt, and pepper.
2. Warm the tortilla and spread tahini sauce in the center.
3. Add rice, black beans, and the mushroom-kale mixture.
4. Roll up the burrito tightly and serve.

## Mexican Rice and Bean Wrap

**Ingredients:**

- 1 large flour tortilla
- 1/2 cup cooked Mexican rice
- 1/4 cup black beans, rinsed and drained
- 1/4 cup corn kernels
- 1/4 cup diced tomatoes
- 1/4 cup shredded lettuce
- 1 tbsp salsa
- 1 tbsp sour cream (optional)
- 1/4 tsp cumin
- 1/4 tsp chili powder
- Salt and pepper to taste

**Instructions:**

1. In a bowl, combine cooked rice, black beans, corn, diced tomatoes, cumin, chili powder, salt, and pepper.
2. Warm the tortilla and spread salsa and sour cream (if using) in the center.
3. Add the rice and bean mixture, followed by shredded lettuce.
4. Roll up the wrap and slice in half.

## Tempeh Bacon and Avocado Wrap

**Ingredients:**

- **1 large flour tortilla**
- **1/2 cup tempeh bacon**, cooked
- **1/2 avocado**, sliced
- **1/4 cup spinach leaves**
- **1/4 cup shredded carrots**
- **1 tbsp tahini sauce**
- **1 tsp lemon juice**
- **Salt and pepper** to taste

**Instructions:**

1. Cook tempeh bacon according to package instructions.
2. Warm the tortilla and spread tahini sauce and lemon juice in the center.
3. Layer with tempeh bacon, avocado, spinach, and shredded carrots.
4. Season with salt and pepper, then roll up the wrap and serve.

## Falafel Wrap with Tzatziki

**Ingredients:**

- 1 **large flour tortilla**
- **3-4 falafel balls**, warmed
- **1/4 cup cucumber**, diced
- **1/4 cup tomatoes**, diced
- **1/4 cup red onion**, thinly sliced
- **1/4 cup lettuce**, shredded
- **2 tbsp tzatziki sauce**
- **1 tbsp fresh parsley**, chopped
- **Salt and pepper** to taste

**Instructions:**

1. Warm the falafel balls and prepare the tzatziki sauce.
2. Warm the tortilla and spread tzatziki sauce in the center.
3. Add falafel, cucumber, tomatoes, onion, lettuce, and parsley.
4. Season with salt and pepper, then roll up the wrap and serve.

## Grilled Portobello Mushroom Burrito

**Ingredients:**

- 1 large flour tortilla
- **1-2 large Portobello mushrooms,** grilled and sliced
- 1/4 cup cooked quinoa
- **1/4 cup black beans**, rinsed and drained
- 1/4 cup corn kernels
- 1/4 cup diced red onion
- 1 tbsp salsa
- **1 tbsp sour cream** (optional)
- 1/4 tsp smoked paprika
- **Salt and pepper** to taste

**Instructions:**

1. Grill and slice the Portobello mushrooms.
2. Warm the tortilla and spread salsa and sour cream (if using) in the center.
3. Layer the quinoa, black beans, corn, red onion, and grilled mushrooms.
4. Sprinkle with smoked paprika, salt, and pepper, then roll up the burrito tightly.

## Peanut Butter and Banana Wrap

**Ingredients:**

- 1 **large flour tortilla**
- 2 **tbsp peanut butter**
- 1 **banana**, sliced
- 1 **tbsp honey** (optional)
- 1/4 **tsp cinnamon** (optional)

**Instructions:**

1. Warm the tortilla slightly to make it more pliable.
2. Spread peanut butter evenly across the center of the tortilla.
3. Layer with banana slices, drizzle with honey, and sprinkle with cinnamon.
4. Roll up the tortilla and slice in half for serving.

## Sweet Potato, Quinoa, and Black Bean Wrap

**Ingredients:**

- 1 large flour tortilla
- **1/2 cup roasted sweet potato**, diced
- **1/4 cup cooked quinoa**
- **1/4 cup black beans**, rinsed and drained
- 1/4 cup spinach leaves
- 1 tbsp tahini sauce
- 1 tbsp lime juice
- **Salt and pepper** to taste

**Instructions:**

1. Roast the sweet potatoes until tender.
2. Warm the tortilla and drizzle tahini sauce and lime juice in the center.
3. Add quinoa, black beans, spinach, and roasted sweet potato.
4. Season with salt and pepper, roll up the wrap, and serve.

## Curry Chickpea Wrap

**Ingredients:**

- 1 large flour tortilla
- 1/2 cup cooked chickpeas
- 1/4 cup diced cucumber
- 1/4 cup shredded carrots
- 1 tbsp curry powder
- 1 tbsp tahini sauce
- 1 tbsp lemon juice
- 1 tbsp fresh cilantro, chopped
- **Salt and pepper** to taste

**Instructions:**

1. In a bowl, toss chickpeas with curry powder, salt, and pepper.
2. Warm the tortilla and drizzle tahini sauce and lemon juice in the center.
3. Add the chickpeas, cucumber, carrots, and fresh cilantro.
4. Roll up the wrap and serve.

## Avocado and Cucumber Sushi Roll Wrap

**Ingredients:**

- **1 large seaweed sheet** (nori)
- **1/2 avocado**, sliced
- **1/4 cucumber**, julienned
- **1/4 cup cooked rice** (preferably sushi rice)
- **1 tbsp soy sauce**
- **1/2 tsp sesame seeds**
- **1 tsp rice vinegar** (optional)

**Instructions:**

1. Lay the seaweed sheet on a flat surface.
2. Spread a thin layer of rice along the center of the nori.
3. Add avocado slices and cucumber strips on top of the rice.
4. Drizzle with soy sauce and a little rice vinegar (optional), then sprinkle with sesame seeds.
5. Roll tightly and slice into pieces. Serve with additional soy sauce on the side.

## Cauliflower Buffalo Wrap

**Ingredients:**

- **1 large flour tortilla**
- **1/2 cup cauliflower florets**, roasted and tossed in buffalo sauce
- **1/4 cup shredded lettuce**
- **1 tbsp ranch dressing** (optional)
- **1/4 cup shredded carrots**
- **1 tbsp blue cheese crumbles** (optional)

**Instructions:**

1. Roast the cauliflower florets until crispy, then toss them in buffalo sauce.
2. Warm the tortilla and layer with shredded lettuce, carrots, and cauliflower.
3. Drizzle with ranch dressing and sprinkle with blue cheese, if desired.
4. Roll up the wrap tightly and serve.

## Zucchini and Hummus Wrap

**Ingredients:**

- 1 large flour tortilla
- **1/2 zucchini**, thinly sliced and grilled
- **2 tbsp hummus**
- **1/4 cup spinach leaves**
- **1/4 cup shredded carrots**
- **1 tbsp lemon juice**
- **Salt and pepper** to taste

**Instructions:**

1. Grill or sauté zucchini slices until tender.
2. Spread hummus evenly on the center of the tortilla.
3. Add zucchini, spinach, shredded carrots, and drizzle with lemon juice.
4. Season with salt and pepper, then roll up the wrap and serve.

## Eggplant and Tomato Burrito

**Ingredients:**

- 1 large flour tortilla
- **1/2 eggplant**, sliced and grilled
- **1/4 cup diced tomatoes**
- **1/4 cup cooked quinoa**
- **1 tbsp tahini sauce**
- **1 tbsp fresh basil**, chopped
- **Salt and pepper** to taste

**Instructions:**

1. Grill the eggplant slices until tender.
2. Warm the tortilla and drizzle tahini sauce in the center.
3. Add quinoa, grilled eggplant, diced tomatoes, and fresh basil.
4. Season with salt and pepper, then roll up the burrito and serve.

**Spicy Sriracha Tofu Wrap**

**Ingredients:**

- 1 large flour tortilla
- **1/2 block tofu**, pressed and sliced
- **1 tbsp sriracha sauce**
- **1/4 cup shredded cabbage**
- **1/4 cup cucumber**, sliced
- **1 tbsp soy sauce**
- **1/4 tsp sesame seeds**

**Instructions:**

1. Press the tofu to remove excess water, then slice it into strips.
2. Sauté the tofu with sriracha sauce and soy sauce until golden and crispy.
3. Warm the tortilla and layer with sautéed tofu, shredded cabbage, and cucumber.
4. Sprinkle with sesame seeds and roll up the wrap. Serve with extra sriracha if desired.

**Rice Paper Veggie Wrap**

**Ingredients:**

- **4 rice paper sheets**
- **1/4 cup shredded carrots**
- **1/4 cup cucumber**, julienned
- **1/4 cup avocado**, sliced
- **1/4 cup fresh herbs** (like cilantro or mint)
- **2 tbsp peanut dipping sauce**

**Instructions:**

1. Soak the rice paper sheets in warm water for a few seconds until soft.
2. Place each sheet on a flat surface and layer with shredded carrots, cucumber, avocado, and fresh herbs.
3. Fold the sides in, then roll tightly to seal the wrap.
4. Serve with peanut dipping sauce on the side.

## Tofu Scramble and Avocado Wrap

**Ingredients:**

- **1 large flour tortilla**
- **1/2 block firm tofu**, crumbled
- **1/4 avocado**, sliced
- **1/4 cup sautéed spinach**
- **1/4 cup diced tomatoes**
- **1 tbsp nutritional yeast** (optional)
- **Salt and pepper** to taste

**Instructions:**

1. Crumble the tofu into a pan and cook it with a bit of olive oil until it resembles scrambled eggs. Add spinach and sauté until wilted.
2. Warm the tortilla and layer with tofu scramble, avocado, and diced tomatoes.
3. Sprinkle with nutritional yeast (if using), salt, and pepper, then roll up the wrap and serve.

## Grilled Corn and Avocado Burrito

**Ingredients:**

- 1 large flour tortilla
- **1 ear of corn**, grilled and kernels removed
- **1/4 avocado**, sliced
- **1/4 cup cooked rice**
- **1/4 cup black beans**, rinsed and drained
- **1 tbsp lime juice**
- **Salt and pepper** to taste

**Instructions:**

1. Grill the corn and remove the kernels.
2. Warm the tortilla and layer with rice, black beans, grilled corn, and avocado.
3. Drizzle with lime juice, season with salt and pepper, then roll up the burrito and serve.

# Roasted Butternut Squash Wrap

**Ingredients:**

- 1 large flour tortilla
- 1/2 butternut squash, peeled and cubed
- 1/4 cup cooked quinoa
- 1 tbsp olive oil
- 1 tsp ground cumin
- 1 tsp smoked paprika
- 1/4 cup arugula
- 1/4 cup tahini sauce
- **Salt and pepper** to taste

**Instructions:**

1. Preheat the oven to 400°F (200°C). Toss butternut squash cubes with olive oil, cumin, paprika, salt, and pepper.
2. Roast for 25-30 minutes or until tender and slightly caramelized.
3. Warm the tortilla and layer with cooked quinoa, roasted squash, arugula, and tahini sauce.
4. Roll up the wrap and serve.

## Cabbage and Carrot Slaw Wrap

**Ingredients:**

- **1 large flour tortilla**
- **1/2 cup shredded cabbage**
- **1/2 cup shredded carrots**
- **1/4 cup fresh cilantro**, chopped
- **2 tbsp rice vinegar**
- **1 tbsp sesame oil**
- **1 tsp honey** (optional)
- **Salt and pepper** to taste

**Instructions:**

1. In a bowl, toss cabbage, carrots, and cilantro.
2. In a separate bowl, whisk together rice vinegar, sesame oil, honey, salt, and pepper.
3. Pour the dressing over the slaw and toss to coat.
4. Warm the tortilla and fill with the cabbage slaw mixture.
5. Roll up the wrap and serve.

## Asian-Inspired Peanut Noodle Wrap

**Ingredients:**

- 1 large flour tortilla
- 1/2 cup cooked noodles (e.g., soba or rice noodles)
- 1/4 cup peanut butter
- 1 tbsp soy sauce
- 1 tbsp rice vinegar
- 1 tsp sesame oil
- **1/4 cup cucumber**, julienned
- 1/4 cup shredded carrots
- 1 tbsp sesame seeds

**Instructions:**

1. In a bowl, mix peanut butter, soy sauce, rice vinegar, and sesame oil to make the sauce.
2. Toss the cooked noodles with the peanut sauce until well coated.
3. Warm the tortilla and layer with the peanut noodles, cucumber, and carrots.
4. Sprinkle with sesame seeds, roll up the wrap, and serve.

## Chickpea Salad Wrap

**Ingredients:**

- 1 large flour tortilla
- **1/2 cup cooked chickpeas**, mashed
- **1/4 cup diced cucumber**
- **1/4 cup diced tomatoes**
- **1/4 cup red onion**, thinly sliced
- **2 tbsp tahini**
- **1 tbsp lemon juice**
- **Salt and pepper** to taste

**Instructions:**

1. Mash the chickpeas with a fork or potato masher in a bowl.
2. Add cucumber, tomatoes, red onion, tahini, lemon juice, salt, and pepper. Stir to combine.
3. Warm the tortilla and layer with the chickpea salad mixture.
4. Roll up the wrap and serve.

## Vegan Caesar Salad Wrap

**Ingredients:**

- **1 large flour tortilla**
- **1 cup romaine lettuce**, chopped
- **2 tbsp vegan Caesar dressing**
- **1 tbsp nutritional yeast**
- **1/4 cup croutons** (optional)

**Instructions:**

1. Toss chopped romaine lettuce with vegan Caesar dressing and nutritional yeast.
2. Warm the tortilla and layer with the Caesar salad mixture.
3. Add croutons if desired, then roll up the wrap and serve.

## Avocado and Mango Burrito

**Ingredients:**

- **1 large flour tortilla**
- **1/2 avocado**, sliced
- **1/2 mango**, diced
- **1/4 cup black beans**, rinsed and drained
- **1/4 cup rice**
- **1 tbsp lime juice**
- **Salt and pepper** to taste

**Instructions:**

1. Warm the tortilla and layer with rice, black beans, avocado, and mango.
2. Drizzle with lime juice, season with salt and pepper, then roll up the burrito and serve.

## Grilled Tempeh and Arugula Wrap

**Ingredients:**

- 1 large flour tortilla
- **1/2 block tempeh,** sliced and grilled
- 1/4 cup arugula
- **1 tbsp balsamic vinegar**
- **1 tbsp olive oil**
- **Salt and pepper** to taste

**Instructions:**

1. Grill tempeh slices until crispy and golden.
2. Warm the tortilla and drizzle with balsamic vinegar and olive oil.
3. Layer with grilled tempeh and arugula. Season with salt and pepper.
4. Roll up the wrap and serve.

## Thai Peanut Veggie Burrito

**Ingredients:**

- 1 large flour tortilla
- 1/4 cup peanut butter
- 1 tbsp soy sauce
- 1 tbsp lime juice
- 1 tsp sesame oil
- 1/4 cup shredded carrots
- 1/4 cup **cucumber**, julienned
- 1/4 cup **bell pepper**, thinly sliced
- 1 tbsp **cilantro**, chopped

**Instructions:**

1. In a bowl, mix peanut butter, soy sauce, lime juice, and sesame oil to make the peanut sauce.
2. Warm the tortilla and drizzle with peanut sauce.
3. Add shredded carrots, cucumber, bell pepper, and cilantro.
4. Roll up the burrito and serve.

# Vegan "Chicken" Caesar Wrap

**Ingredients:**

- 1 large flour tortilla
- 1/2 cup vegan "chicken" strips
- **1 cup romaine lettuce**, chopped
- **2 tbsp vegan Caesar dressing**
- **1 tbsp nutritional yeast**
- **1/4 cup croutons** (optional)

**Instructions:**

1. Warm the vegan "chicken" strips according to package instructions.
2. Toss romaine lettuce with vegan Caesar dressing and nutritional yeast.
3. Warm the tortilla and layer with the "chicken" strips and Caesar salad mixture.
4. Add croutons if desired, then roll up the wrap and serve.

## Moroccan-Spiced Chickpea Burrito

**Ingredients:**

- 1 large flour tortilla
- 1/2 cup cooked chickpeas
- 1 tbsp olive oil
- 1 tsp cumin
- 1 tsp paprika
- 1/2 tsp cinnamon
- 1/4 tsp turmeric
- 1/4 cup couscous (or rice)
- 1/4 cup fresh cilantro, chopped
- 1/4 cup plain yogurt (optional, for topping)
- **Salt and pepper** to taste

**Instructions:**

1. Heat olive oil in a pan and add cooked chickpeas. Stir in cumin, paprika, cinnamon, turmeric, salt, and pepper. Cook for 5-7 minutes until fragrant.
2. Warm the tortilla and layer with couscous, spiced chickpeas, and cilantro.
3. Drizzle with yogurt if desired, then roll up the burrito and serve.

## Mushroom and Spinach Wrap

**Ingredients:**

- **1 large flour tortilla**
- **1 cup mushrooms**, sliced
- **1/2 cup spinach**, fresh
- **1 tbsp olive oil**
- **1/4 cup hummus**
- **1 tbsp balsamic vinegar**
- **1/4 cup feta cheese** (optional)
- **Salt and pepper** to taste

**Instructions:**

1. Heat olive oil in a pan and sauté mushrooms until tender, about 5 minutes. Add spinach and balsamic vinegar, and cook until spinach wilts.
2. Warm the tortilla and spread a thin layer of hummus.
3. Add the sautéed mushrooms and spinach, then sprinkle with feta cheese (if using).
4. Roll up the wrap and serve.

## Avocado, Bean, and Corn Wrap

**Ingredients:**

- **1 large flour tortilla**
- **1/2 avocado**, sliced
- **1/4 cup black beans**, rinsed and drained
- **1/4 cup corn kernels**
- **1/4 cup diced tomatoes**
- **1 tbsp lime juice**
- **1/4 cup fresh cilantro**, chopped
- **Salt and pepper** to taste

**Instructions:**

1. Warm the tortilla and layer with avocado, black beans, corn, and diced tomatoes.
2. Drizzle with lime juice and sprinkle with cilantro, salt, and pepper.
3. Roll up the wrap and serve.

## Zesty Lime and Quinoa Burrito

**Ingredients:**

- 1 large flour tortilla
- 1/2 cup cooked quinoa
- 1/4 cup **black beans**, rinsed and drained
- 1/4 cup corn kernels
- 1/4 cup diced tomatoes
- 1 tbsp lime juice
- 1/4 tsp chili powder
- 1/4 cup **fresh cilantro**, chopped
- **Salt and pepper** to taste

**Instructions:**

1. Warm the tortilla and layer with cooked quinoa, black beans, corn, and diced tomatoes.
2. Drizzle with lime juice, sprinkle with chili powder, and garnish with cilantro.
3. Season with salt and pepper, then roll up the burrito and serve.

## Mediterranean Veggie Wrap

**Ingredients:**

- 1 large flour tortilla
- 1/4 cup hummus
- **1/4 cup cucumber**, sliced
- **1/4 cup red bell pepper**, thinly sliced
- **1/4 cup red onion**, thinly sliced
- **1/4 cup Kalamata olives**, chopped
- 1/4 cup spinach or lettuce
- 1 tbsp olive oil
- 1 tsp lemon juice
- **Salt and pepper** to taste

**Instructions:**

1. Warm the tortilla and spread a layer of hummus.
2. Layer with cucumber, bell pepper, red onion, olives, and spinach.
3. Drizzle with olive oil and lemon juice, and season with salt and pepper.
4. Roll up the wrap and serve.

## Sweet and Sour Tofu Wrap

**Ingredients:**

- **1 large flour tortilla**
- **1/2 block firm tofu**, pressed and cubed
- **1/4 cup sweet and sour sauce**
- **1/4 cup shredded carrots**
- **1/4 cup cucumber**, julienned
- **1/4 cup lettuce or cabbage**, shredded
- **1 tbsp olive oil**
- **Salt and pepper** to taste

**Instructions:**

1. Heat olive oil in a pan and sauté tofu cubes until golden and crispy, about 5-7 minutes.
2. Stir in sweet and sour sauce and cook for another 2-3 minutes.
3. Warm the tortilla and layer with the tofu mixture, shredded carrots, cucumber, and lettuce.
4. Roll up the wrap and serve.

## Lemon Herb Tofu Wrap

**Ingredients:**

- **1 large flour tortilla**
- **1/2 block firm tofu**, pressed and sliced
- **1 tbsp olive oil**
- **1 tsp lemon zest**
- **1 tbsp fresh lemon juice**
- **1 tbsp fresh herbs** (e.g., parsley, thyme, or basil), chopped
- **1/4 cup spinach or lettuce**
- **Salt and pepper** to taste

**Instructions:**

1. Heat olive oil in a pan and sauté tofu slices until golden, about 5-7 minutes.
2. Stir in lemon zest, lemon juice, fresh herbs, salt, and pepper.
3. Warm the tortilla and layer with the tofu, spinach or lettuce.
4. Roll up the wrap and serve.

## Spicy Pinto Bean and Avocado Wrap

**Ingredients:**

- **1 large flour tortilla**
- **1/2 cup pinto beans**, mashed
- **1/2 avocado**, sliced
- **1/4 cup salsa**
- **1/4 cup shredded lettuce**
- **1/4 tsp chili powder**
- **1 tbsp lime juice**
- **Salt and pepper** to taste

**Instructions:**

1. Warm the tortilla and layer with mashed pinto beans.
2. Add avocado slices, salsa, shredded lettuce, and a sprinkle of chili powder.
3. Drizzle with lime juice, season with salt and pepper, and roll up the wrap.
4. Serve immediately.

## Grilled Veggie and Hummus Wrap

**Ingredients:**

- 1 large flour tortilla
- 1/2 cup hummus
- **1/4 cup zucchini**, thinly sliced
- **1/4 cup bell pepper**, thinly sliced
- **1/4 cup red onion**, thinly sliced
- **1/4 cup eggplant**, thinly sliced
- 1 tbsp olive oil
- 1 tsp balsamic vinegar
- 1/4 cup fresh spinach
- **Salt and pepper** to taste

**Instructions:**

1. Heat olive oil in a pan or grill and cook zucchini, bell pepper, red onion, and eggplant until tender and lightly charred.
2. Drizzle with balsamic vinegar, season with salt and pepper.
3. Warm the tortilla and spread a layer of hummus.
4. Add the grilled veggies and fresh spinach, then roll up the wrap and serve.

# Tempeh and Kale Wrap with Mustard Dressing

**Ingredients:**

- **1 large flour tortilla**
- **1/2 block tempeh**, sliced
- **1/2 cup kale**, chopped
- **1 tbsp olive oil**
- **1 tbsp Dijon mustard**
- **1 tbsp maple syrup**
- **1 tsp apple cider vinegar**
- **Salt and pepper** to taste

**Instructions:**

1. Sauté the tempeh in olive oil until golden and crispy, about 5 minutes.
2. In a small bowl, whisk together Dijon mustard, maple syrup, apple cider vinegar, salt, and pepper to make the dressing.
3. Toss kale with a little bit of the mustard dressing.
4. Warm the tortilla and layer with tempeh and dressed kale.
5. Drizzle with additional dressing if desired, then roll up the wrap and serve.

## Vegan BLT Wrap

**Ingredients:**

- 1 large flour tortilla
- **1/2 cup tempeh bacon** or **vegan bacon strips**
- **1/4 cup lettuce**, shredded
- **1/4 cup tomato**, thinly sliced
- **1 tbsp vegan mayo**
- **1 tbsp Dijon mustard**
- **Salt and pepper** to taste

**Instructions:**

1. Cook tempeh bacon or vegan bacon strips according to package instructions.
2. Mix vegan mayo and Dijon mustard together.
3. Warm the tortilla and spread a thin layer of the mayo-mustard mixture.
4. Add the tempeh bacon, lettuce, and tomato.
5. Season with salt and pepper, then roll up the wrap and serve.

## Sweet Potato and Kale Burrito

**Ingredients:**

- **1 large flour tortilla**
- **1 medium sweet potato**, peeled and diced
- **1/2 cup kale**, chopped
- **1 tbsp olive oil**
- **1 tsp cumin**
- **1/2 tsp paprika**
- **1 tbsp lime juice**
- **1/4 cup avocado**, sliced
- **Salt and pepper** to taste

**Instructions:**

1. Preheat oven to 400°F (200°C). Toss diced sweet potato with olive oil, cumin, paprika, salt, and pepper. Roast for 20-25 minutes until tender.
2. Sauté kale in a pan for 3-4 minutes until wilted, and season with salt and pepper.
3. Warm the tortilla and layer with roasted sweet potato, sautéed kale, avocado, and a drizzle of lime juice.
4. Roll up the burrito and serve.

**Chickpea and Avocado Wrap**

**Ingredients:**

- **1 large flour tortilla**
- **1/2 cup chickpeas**, mashed
- **1/2 avocado**, sliced
- **1 tbsp tahini**
- **1 tbsp lemon juice**
- **1/4 cup cucumber**, sliced
- **1/4 cup tomato**, diced
- **Salt and pepper** to taste

**Instructions:**

1. In a bowl, mash chickpeas with tahini, lemon juice, salt, and pepper.
2. Warm the tortilla and spread the mashed chickpea mixture in the center.
3. Add avocado slices, cucumber, and tomato.
4. Roll up the wrap and serve.

## Vegan BBQ Seitan Wrap

**Ingredients:**

- **1 large flour tortilla**
- **1/2 cup seitan**, sliced
- **1/4 cup BBQ sauce**
- **1/4 cup coleslaw**
- **1/4 cup pickles**, sliced
- **1 tbsp olive oil**
- **Salt and pepper** to taste

**Instructions:**

1. Heat olive oil in a pan and sauté seitan slices until crispy, about 5-7 minutes.
2. Stir in BBQ sauce and cook for another 2 minutes until seitan is coated.
3. Warm the tortilla and layer with BBQ seitan, coleslaw, and pickles.
4. Roll up the wrap and serve.

## Avocado, Tomato, and Chickpea Wrap

**Ingredients:**

- **1 large flour tortilla**
- **1/2 avocado**, sliced
- **1/4 cup chickpeas**, mashed
- **1/4 cup tomato**, diced
- **1 tbsp olive oil**
- **1 tbsp lemon juice**
- **1/4 tsp paprika**
- **Salt and pepper** to taste

**Instructions:**

1. In a bowl, mash chickpeas with olive oil, lemon juice, paprika, salt, and pepper.
2. Warm the tortilla and spread the chickpea mixture in the center.
3. Add avocado slices and diced tomato.
4. Roll up the wrap and serve.

## Mango Salsa and Black Bean Burrito

**Ingredients:**

- 1 large flour tortilla
- **1/2 cup black beans**, rinsed and drained
- **1/2 cup mango salsa** (store-bought or homemade)
- **1/4 cup avocado**, sliced
- **1/4 cup corn kernels**
- **1 tbsp lime juice**
- **Salt and pepper** to taste

**Instructions:**

1. Warm the tortilla and layer with black beans, mango salsa, avocado, and corn.
2. Drizzle with lime juice and season with salt and pepper.
3. Roll up the burrito and serve.